He's the Amazing Dream That Came True

He's the Amazing Dream That Came True

Donniece Greene-Smith
With words from Matthew Nathaniel Smith

Copyright 2011 Donniece Greene-Smith

ISBN 978-0-9568357-0-3

Published by Beginners Publishing House

This book is dedicated to my wonderful husband, Matthew. I'm forever thankful you walked out of heaven just to be here with me. Darling, you will always be my dream come true.

Thank you, Matthew, for your words in this book and in my life. They have brought me so much inspiration and encouragement. I'm so glad we are climbing, flying, and touching the sky together. I love you!

I am also eternally thankful and grateful to God for everything!

Thank you to my daughters, Donelle and Li-en. You girls bring so much joy to my life, and you amaze me every day. I write this book for you as well. That way, you know you also deserve the best. Never settle for less.

Thank you to my mom, who has been a huge supporter of everything I've ever done. Thank you for cheering me on all my life.

I'd also like to thank every soul who has crossed my path in some way. Each and every person I've met has played a part in my life. However short that role, I am thankful.

Contents

Introduction ix
Make Me More Beautiful 1
I Feel Beautiful 4
It's True 6
The Balance of Me 7
My Man-to-Be 9
A Dance and a Fantasy 11
Can You Imagine You and Me? 13
I Can Feel Him, but I Can't See Him 15
He's Gotta Dance with Me 18
Baby, Climb with Me 20
Make Him More Beautiful 22
For Matthew, My Friend 25
You Want Love, Don't You…? 27
Matthew's Response to "Baby, Climb with Me" 30
Matthew's Response to "Make Him More Beautiful" ... 31
You Are Oh So Beautiful 32
His Assurance 34
He Comforts Me 35
He Believes in Me 37
My Wedding Night 39

Matthew's Response to "My Wedding Night": First Night with a Queen 41

I'm Lifted Up on Wings 43

He Calls Me Up Higher.. 45

Hey, You.. 47

His Eyes Compose the Scores................................. 50

She Hears a Whisper in the Wind......................... 52

I Flew Past Your Heart Today 53

Going Heights with You 54

Come with Me 56

Every Moment with You... 60

I'm Gonna Love You Now 61

Of All the Days with You.. 62

At Long Last, Your Arms Found Me 63

Your Love.. 65

With Love You Always Win................................... 66

Introduction

It all started with a prayer and a deep desire to experience love as I've always dreamed it to be. I've always believed most of my adult experiences came down to the cards life dealt me and how well I managed them—when, in truth, I had a part to play in the cards that were dealt to me—until one day I found myself at a place feeling there was much more to it. I now believe that I play a huge part in what happens to me and I no longer believe I'm at the mercy of cards that life will deal to me. For years I had exercised my belief in God through prayer, but I didn't experience the fruits of those prayers. I grew quite weary until I learned that it is not what happens to me but how I respond to those things that happen to me that affect the quality of my life. I attributed the quality of my life down to a decision God had made and at times removed the responsibility from myself. After much reflection, I realised I needed to make a change. A change in the opinion I had of myself. I also needed to change my opinion about the mistakes I made in life and the decisions that had brought me to that point.

It took some years to fully look in the mirror and accept the things that had occurred in my life. During this challenging time, I lost my daughter, which brought its own struggles. My daughter Maya died suddenly and of natural causes. It took us all by surprised and turned my world and belief systems inside out. I found it hard to cope with life and at times wanted to end my life. I never knew such grief existed. I couldn't believe I found myself in this place. I thought I was moving forward with life and then that happened. Yet having reached the stage where

I knew things needed to change in my life, I was determined not to allow any negative thinking about life to rob me of the things I really wanted to experience in life. It was important for me not to begin to process things in a way that would hurt me further. This took some time though but I knew the day would come when I would finally be able to say, "Yesterday is over, and today is a new day"—and really mean it. Of course, I'd said that before, but I lived with the self-judgment of my past every single day. I also lived with the judgments of others—but not anymore. One of my poems, "Make Me More Beautiful", which I recited very often, became a personal mantra. As I recited this poem, I felt inner healing taking place as I cried those words I still say today, "Make Me More Beautiful". Something amazing was happening to me.

I was unveiling everything that hindered me. I was, for the first time in my life, free. It slipped into my consciousness that every day was my chance to become more beautiful. From then on, I was determined to feel great about myself and all my experiences in life, both good and bad. It felt amazing, because I could sense this great feeling was happening naturally. I felt good about the experiences I knew I was now intending to have. I felt great about my desires and what I wanted to achieve in life. I felt great about my personality. I felt great about what I wanted to give to this world, and although I had always had a passion for helping others, I could see I was becoming more effective, and this made me feel good about the person I was developing into. I felt so good that it seemed as if my whole being was in constant flight. I felt good things happening to me. No longer did I think, I hope nothing bad happens or what if this or that happens? I no longer felt trapped. I was free! I was free to think and believe all good things could happen for me and to me.

I refused to accept statistics about my age, colour, prospects, or circumstances. In fact, I stopped listening to people who had those limits on themselves and others. It was as if it all became clear. My previous thoughts and beliefs about myself had a direct effect on my life. Now I not only have faith that God wishes to see me happy and blessed, but I believe I am meant to be no other way.

The process of falling in love was so natural, and I could clearly see the things God wanted for me. It was then my prayers became light and full of faith. If I became stuck with something or needed help, it always turned out God had already provided the answer. I began to see answers before I asked the question.

One day, after much turmoil about what was right and wrong regarding love, I clearly remember saying, "Enough is enough! Father, you know what is best for me, and you know more than I do. I wish for you to direct my every thought where love is concerned. Lead me, because although I feel I know what's best for me, I need your help." Almost as soon as I prayed that prayer, I got a vision, and I began writing it down. Every day, I would look at the vision of this man, and I would thank God for him.

This is where the story comes in about He's the Amazing Dream That Came True. I got so many visions of my husband that I started to write about it through one of my passions, poetry. These poems began to flow, and things became clearer and clearer. I started to recite these poems at Beginners Poetry Event Nights which we held weekly, and everyone there could feel the energy coming through these poems. It was as if this man was already there. I could see how we were together as a couple. For the first time in my life, I thought about what I wanted to give this man who was not yet in my life rather than what void he would fill. I wasn't concerned about looks, and I wasn't concerned about what he had or did for a living. I was completely unattached to all things physical during this time of expectancy. How could I think of those things when something bigger was happening inside me? My heart was totally focused about what I wanted to give to him, but every day I received more and more about him, and every morning and every night, I would thank God for him. I could feel his presence, and I knew it... he was on his way to me.

These poems are not just poems of love. They tell the story of faith in love and how, if you let him, God will work out every detail. Sometimes I still sit in amazement at how every positive vision I ever had of a man has been brought to life in the physical representation of my husband. This story is not just about how my dream came true; it's also about how God knows all things and how his choice is always best. I share these poems with you, the reader, because they are real. My hope is you will experience the life in these poems, and they will encourage those of you who have a dream to keep believing.

Donniece Greene-Smith

This particular poem became a mantra for me. It helped me treat each day as an opportunity to become more beautiful whilst I embraced all that took place in my life.

Make Me More Beautiful

As I awaken from my dreamless sleep
And rise upon my feet
I realise I have another day where my heart still beats
I smile at what's ahead
And ask the day to
Make me more beautiful

Still feeling the pain of yesterday
A broken heart still dominates my head
Feels like my insides are turning
Can't breathe
Looking for a way out... help me!
Whatever you do
Make me more beautiful

I know you've tried to give me manners
Thinking if I was under your thumb
You could control me
Never realising you were
Using cruelty
To silence the spirit... in me
Nevertheless I cry
Make me more beautiful

He's the Amazing Dream That Came True

That's right
I speak to that inner me
The one who recognises
There is more to me
Than the horrible things you have called me
Just to get me to a point where I feel ashamed of me
No, can't be
I'm fighting for me
Make me more beautiful

Pain, speak to me
Let me hear why you have subjected me
Only then will I know the source of thee
And it's then I will seek to remove thee
Using the fire to shape me
The excruciating pain to elevate me
As I fulfil my desire to be
Make me more beautiful

I used to cry myself from moment to moment
Wondering just what would I be
If I sat here, letting every Tom, Dick, or Harry
Allow me, to be
Or for that matter
Decide whether I can be proud of me
Maybe yesterday is gone
When I never knew to whom I belonged
I just agreed to get along
But in my heart, I sang a prayerful song
Lord, make me more beautiful

Yes, that's right
I'm rising above the abuse

Up from the past that
Seemed only to confuse
It's something I consciously choose
For me, my life will end with good news
Around the cemetery, they will say
She chose to win and not to lose
When she cried
Make me more beautiful

I wake up each day
Put away the bad memories of the past
And say
Another moment you won't last
Time to remove the mask
Make me more beautiful

No bitter feelings
Running through my veins
Strictly love
Relieving my pain
Doing my best never to complain
Feeling if this don't kill me
It will strengthen who I am
It's in my philosophy
Make me more beautiful

You may wonder why I say all this
It ain't to impress
Or to knock your life full of stress
I seek only to confess
Living this way has given me rest
With my attitude, I feel quite blessed
Knowing it's 'cause I chose to
Make me more beautiful

I Feel Beautiful

*From the top of my head to the bottom of my feet... I feel incredible
I feel as if I can do the supernatural
In all my thoughts, I'm flying; this plane I'm on is truly spiritual
I'm climbing heights to catch a better view
As more of his glory is revealed, I'm even more grateful
My vision is me running through the colour purple, taking in the flowers
And saying to my Lord, I love you
I appreciate the goodness that has made my life full
Lord, thank you for allowing me to breathe another day
You've been to me so merciful
How can I ever thank you?
Although it hasn't been easy, I appreciate my journey
Knowing you've always been there
Has given me the assurance that my life is purposeful
For me, you had a plan, even when I didn't understand
You've brought me through some of the most painful things, and I can still stand
You called me your daughter and said, "For you, Donniece, I've paved a road, and it has all the things you need to be fulfilled."
In my heart, I scream, "Lord, to me you are so wonderful.
It is you that makes me more beautiful.
How can I ever thank you?"
When I wake in the morning and open my eyes
Do all that you can to reveal the glory that hides*

Donniece Greene-Smith

Let me pass the test
And know with certainty that I've been blessed
For my mind, spirit, and soul has been given rest
My Father, you are truly the best
I'll sing from the mountaintop and confess
My Lord, my Father, is so wonderful, and that is why I feel so beautiful

He's the Amazing Dream That Came True

So it begins. My prayer gives birth to visions...

It's True

It's true
I'm about to embark on the most beautiful road ever made
So it's been said
With anticipation, I run arms opened
In surety that my love will meet you
No doubt it's true
For my reality will only mirror love
With no apologies
Who are you?
You're my absolute dream come true
I won't name you
For I'm allowing life to choose you
So for now, I'll send my love
In a kiss that I just blew
Knowing that you're on this road
I'm assured it will get to you

Donniece Greene-Smith

The Balance of Me

The balance of me
Truly loves me, for he loves himself

The balance of me
Respects me. Why? Because he respects himself

The balance of me
Encourages me, and in doing so encourages himself

The balance of me
Speaks to me, as no other voice can reach where he reaches

The balance of me
Calls me up higher. With a loving voice, he lifts me

The balance of me
Sees my gifts, won't let me forget I came into this world bearing gifts

The balance of me
Corrects me, and whilst he's doing it, I know we're on the same team

The balance of me
Directs me when I'm going the wrong way
He lovingly says, "Baby, it's not that way"

He's the Amazing Dream That Came True

The balance of me
Covers me, giving me assurance with his God-given ability

The balance of me
Looks at me as if God placed me right in his hand

The balance of me
Touches me, and oh my God

The balance of me
Blesses me. After God, he's the first to provide the best

The balance of me
Cares for me, and in my vulnerability, he does all to protect me

The balance of me
Honours me, making sure he never lets me forget how valuable I am

The balance of me
Adores me, letting me know how wonderful I am to him

The balance of me
Loves me completely… full stop

The balance of me
Completes me. What else can I say? He truly balances me.

Donniece Greene-Smith

My Man-To-Be

For the Lord… he got this thing
Makes a girl just wanna sing
Not a stranger to a fall
But knows how to get back up

The passion that runs through his veins
Screams freedom fighter in every way
By his side I'm looking to stay
'Cause in his purpose is
Upliftment for his people in every way

I wanna march for him
Hold up signs, make some tracks,
And bust the charts for him

My man-to-be… is debt-free
And by this I mean he's not afraid to express himself emotionally
This makes him able to love me fearlessly

In everything he strives to have integrity
Knows he was made perfectly
This helps him walk this life effectively

He's the Amazing Dream That Came True

To my young ladies, he'll lead the way
Schooling them lovingly, for when it comes to their day
He knows how to rap to me
His regular conversation is always poetic
And I'll rap back so that he can see
My anticipation is heightened for him always… automatically
Watching him climb… I wanna take to the skies with him

He'll get the best of me
That is a guarantee
Why? Because I'm free finally
No more chains 'round his queen-to-be
I'll stand beside him fearlessly
But for now, I celebrate my liberty
Whilst I wait upon my king… my man-to-be!

Donniece Greene-Smith

A Dance and a Fantasy

I'm ready to take a chance with you
Feeling good about this romance with you
Got me dreaming about a graceful yet sensual dance with you
All of which has just enhanced my mood
To climactic thoughts of you being a part of my daily food
Me loving you as you love me through and through
Man loving his wife, this is exactly what's missing in his life
He wants to play with me
Not my mentality
But a roll-on-the-ground, pillow-fight… type
His body glistens… What? Yeah, I said his body glistens
I can come off track; after all, I'm writing 'bout my fantasy
Yet in my mind he's saying, "Whatcha mean, fantasy?
Baby, you're writing about that place we transcend; it's our destiny
Hold on, don't pull it back, we can make this be
We've got a place in time where we need to be
Where I'm loving you, you're loving me
I'm on the mountaintop…
THANK YA, LORD … for this lovely lady
She's just heavenly
So glad, so glad I prayed and believed
She'd take a chance with me and
Entertained romance with me
THANK YOU, GOD
For getting her to dance that dance with me

He's the Amazing Dream That Came True

*Enhancing the chance of her falling so gracefully
Into what seems like hers, but it's my fantasy"
You're truly awesome, God
How you gave him the same vision you gave me
Who's talking now?
It doesn't matter, boo
You chose me, I chose you
Now come on and share this dance with me.*

Donniece Greene-Smith

Can You Imagine You and Me?

Can you imagine you and me?
Close your eyes
Come take a walk with me
I know it's dark, but in this park
Your heartbeat sparks the lights to beam
Let's talk about your lifelong dreams
I'm thinking we'd make a pretty good team
My aim is to walk through all my dreams
Live out my fantasies
Now back to you and me
Can you feel my desire to be an addition to your being?
So encouraging is my love it spells remarkably
Been given the anointing to make everything I touch more beautiful
With you I'd take love to new heights we've dreamed
To others it would seem like a fantasy
But like I said, I live out my fantasies
Are you my Mr. Me? The double of me
My mirror reflection equals ecstasy
Forgive me as I remind myself there's no need to ask
'Cause you're on this walk with me
We've just pushed through hell, now we walk somewhere heavenly
Assured was I when I blew that kiss
That it would land perfectly
Now this question of you and me
It's been understood that once we've linked

He's the Amazing Dream That Came True

The earth would kiss the moon
The inhabitants would hear a great kaboom
As drippings of love's example
Would spread its secret dew
Giving millions upon millions
A glimpse into a life they never knew
Can you imagine the happiness it would bring if there was a "you and me"?

Donniece Greene-Smith

I Can Feel Him, but I Can't See Him

I can feel him, but I can't see him
That is, physically
His smile is just right
Maybe because every time I see it, he's smiling at me
Whenever I'm doing anything, he's there with me
I see his responses, and it comforts me
"Who are you?" I say with great anticipation
"Who are you?" Come enter this life of mine and make this vision a reality
You're there one moment, and then you are not
Where are you? Stop eluding me… I'm already attracted to you
God help me, sometimes my eyes play tricks on me
I look and focus on the physical exterior
Thinking I know how I'd like him to be
Then those visions become cloudy and out-of-focus; he fades from me
God help me, he's my vision… my dream come true
Still, in my physical world, there's no trace of him, not even a clue
Yet in my visions, there's just so much we seem to do
Baby, can you hear me? I love you
There's no hesitation; when the pastor asks, I'll be the first to say "I do"
I can feel him; it's so real; can this be true?

He's the Amazing Dream That Came True

This man doesn't even know, my mind he just blew
He's got me asking, "Who are you?"
I wanna romance and most definitely dance with you
Still the spirit speaks to me, saying
"He's very near, but his face you can't see"
It's driving me crazy… honestly
Then I close my eyes and go back to the Braille
He gave me a clue
Saying, "Only through the spirit will it be revealed to you"
So when this one came and that one came
I was able to say, "No, it's not you"
I'm so glad I prayed before and asked you to take hold of this
I asked for a guide, one that I just couldn't miss
So although you look so very good
I'm doing my math, and if it don't add up… it ain't you
The other night, I prayed and asked God for clarity
Closed my eyes and a vision came to me
You and I were spiritual, bonded into one
The message at the end was that together the war would be won
Woke up to another sign, or should I say confusion, 'cause I saw a face
Thinking, "Come on, God. Just transcend me to his place"
But then is it you? Is that my clue?
I haven't had the chance to get to know you
Then I hear a voice say, "Not until I see what was shown to me in spirit"
Then the next night comes, and I say again, "Give me clarity"
Woke up frustrated
'Cause, guess what, in my dreams he came to me again
This time he kissed me, then I did awake
Asking God, "Are you playing with me?
Take this man out of my dreams

Donniece Greene-Smith

Here's a piece of paper with my number and address
Come tonight when I ask for clarity
Tell him I'm cooking dinner, and he's my special guest
I'll promise you, Lord, his spirit I'll test.

He's Gotta Dance with Me

Lord, he's gotta dance with me
The desire for this romance is all he sees
I push, Lord, believing with you, Lord, we can have everything
Having settled for average so many times before
Having ignored the dreams that knocked on my door
And many nights screaming with regret
I walk onto that ledge, and I know I'm so close to the edge
But it's been my dream for as long as I could see
His desire is to dance with me and feel the passion running through me
He draws me closer, saying, "Baby, I'm in ecstasy"
I can't believe we've been given the chance to make this be
Hold on to me, let me take the lead, there is something I want you to see
When you were born, you were given a dream
And in this dream, your spirit was shown a glimpse of me
For the appointed time, where you would reach up and grab hold of me
Baby, that's why this dance is a dance for the heavenly
And I know when you prayed for a man who would understand
It was your belief in God that would make this be
For where you've come from and what you went through
It would take an extraordinary determination to push aside everything

Donniece Greene-Smith

And wait on your dream to come true
Well, baby, when you prayed, I also prayed
That you would get the revelation that you were not average
That when you fell asleep, you would dream
And this would keep your spirit awake for when this day would come
When you were strong
Ready to know that on this road is where you belong

Baby, I've been waiting for you and waiting to see me with you
Oh! How tonight, this night, you look so beautiful
Just as I always thought you would
My love, now that we share this dance, and my body is so near to you
You'll feel my heartbeat release the answers to your questions
Just as you requested it to
Seeing the smile on your face has made we want to tighten my embrace
Wow, I'm feeling this is the most beautiful place
I've waited so long, and now there is no time to waste
The ring I've chosen for you awaits its space
My wife, you will be for an eternity
Your husband, I will be in this dream and ultimately our reality
Baby, I loved you then, and I love you now
And I thank God for the dream, which kept you holding on for me.

Baby, Climb with Me

When you talk with me, I wanna feel your dreams
That's how I want you to speak to me
Give me the treasured thoughts that will make you scream
Don't wanna get in your head
Just wanna share those higher states of being
Do you see what I mean?
I want you to climb with me
Reach the emotional sky with me
Fly with me
Whisper sweet somethings as you lie beside me
That way, I know you'll rise for me
Come morning time, anoint the day with me
Trust me
I'm making loving you a reality
One where we can leave behind average and shoot for high expectancy
Come touch the clouds with me
Take me in your arms and grab hold of me
Show me the man you wanna be
I'll receive you hungrily
Loving me won't be a mystery
It'll be easy when you pull on my heartstrings,
Feel my spiritual being
Make love to me mentally
Capture me

Donniece Greene-Smith

Help me see the imagines you dream
Darling, I'm actually talking about living our fantasies
Yes, we can! Yes, we can! Walk in the heavenlies
We can write the pages that tell Love's history
God says it's better if you do it spiritually
Like the blind, we can feel our way, so that we can reap it physically
Do you feel me?
Baby, climb with me; come fly with me; touch the sky with me.

He's the Amazing Dream That Came True

Make Him More Beautiful

As he enters my space
Let it light up my face
Let me feel the warmth from his embrace
Let him know, in my heart, love is placed
Lord, make him beautiful

When he opens his mouth and talks to me
Let the words he breathes nourish me
Let his eyes reflect the glory he sees
Let his manly anointing drip honour and respect on me
Then let him know his loving commands I will receive
Lord, make him beautiful

When he makes a mistake and falls from grace
Give him the humility to seek your face
Let your heart's desires be all that he tastes
Let him understand, Lord, your love had him purposely placed
Make him more beautiful

When he wakes every morning and opens his eyes
Let the sun reveal the glory he hides
And his flesh seek the spirit to revive
Let him know to ask you to put more love inside
Lord, make him more beautiful

Donniece Greene-Smith

When he opens the door
And exits our place
Let the kiss I give him strengthen his pace
Assuring him, his loving return I eagerly await
His dinner's ready, now there's no time to waste
Please hold me, darling, as only you can with your sweet embrace
Now, Lord, make this part beautiful

As I close my eyes
And softly kiss his lips
Let me feel the shivers
As they send signals to my hips
Making him much more beautiful

Look at your legs; they look so strong
Let them lead me to where we belong
'Cause right now, I'm hearing a million love songs
No need to ask if I'm ready, baby
Trust me, I've been waiting for you all day long
Make this even more beautiful

I've got God's love just the way he intended it for you
Hungrily awaiting, anticipating
Visions of a life, meditating on how I'm gonna love you
'Cause you are, you are oh so beautiful
Satisfying me won't be a problem for you

He's the Amazing Dream That Came True

*As I was half done before we'd even begun
'Cause he made you so damn beautiful
I'm thinking I'm so glad I married you
Lord, thank you for making him beautiful*

Donniece Greene-Smith

Meeting Matthew

Matthew and I met at a birthday party, but there was nothing unusual about our meeting. Nothing happened to tell me he was the one for me. Although I was open to meeting this man of my visions just about anywhere, I wanted to remain unattached, and I did that by not focusing on individuals. For the first time in my life, I was going to allow my spirit to lead the way. Unknown to me at the time, Matthew had been waiting to meet his wife all of his adult life. All I could do was encourage him to continue to believe he would meet her.

For Matthew, My Friend

My friend... Lord, I pray you bless him
Set him up for life... bestow upon him the beauty and grace of a loving wife
Come on, my Lord... shower him
Bring your stars into view
He's done all he could think of and all he could possibly do
Putting you first as you told him to
Now he's weary, sometimes wondering... why he should lean on you
Knowing you are the Almighty,
Knowing from you extends all truth
Leaves him somewhat confused at this point in time, but
Breaking your commands, he's not willing to do

He's the Amazing Dream That Came True

Open our eyes, Lord, to the treasures that lie before us
Encourage his heart to look for love again
But this time, let there actually be an exchange of wedding rings
I cry out to you, Lord, because I believe
Please open his understanding so his dream he can conceive
Fill his heart with the passion he will give and also receive
As I pray this, Lord, let your wisdom in this be perceived
Restore his desires. Let him look, knowing he will find
Let your angels be sent on this one thing… let them be assigned
Bring him a rose from your garden
One that would make any man smile
Let all things be fruitful through to the birth of their child
Lord, I know my friend loves you so much
That's why I'm crying out for you to bless him
Give him the experience of his faithful wife's touch
This poetic prayer I send up to you
Is, without a doubt, my heartfelt tears
For a man who's waiting on you, but sometimes finds it hard to bear

Donniece Greene-Smith

You Want Love, Don't You...?

Maybe it was at first glance
That his heart began to dance
His curious thoughts brought him closer, wondering
What is this... my eyes have been blessed to see?
My thoughts. You want love, don't you?
Filled with the message of love to all who'd give an ear
I stood in my pulpit of love like Cupid and spoke melodies he longed to hear
Come with me, let me show you the road that God showed me
It's filled with all the joys that a man and woman could ever dream
Yet fear has deceived you, so it would seem
If I can give you my eyes for a moment
I'd show you the most beautiful scene

My friend, I see the love of your life making an entrance
And this love will encourage you to change your whole being
She says, "You want love, don't you?"
Little did she know, as she spoke the words the spirit had given to her,
You held onto the voice that God was using
Even though, when she spoke, it was not just to you
The thought entered your mind, "What if she is all that I wanted?"
Captured by the words she uttered
More than got your heart to flutter

But little did she know
So she says with the purity of her heart
Believing, encouraging you in love
Would put a smile on your and God's heart
She said, "In you, I see a passion for love, if only you believed"
You being loved in ways
You're afraid to tell anyone you've dreamed
She says, "You want love, don't you?"

There's a woman out there for you
Look closely. Can you see what I see?
She recognises you for the man that God called you to be
That's all she sees… just believe
She wants her kiss to give you new pleasures with every release
She wants her touch to bring you ecstasy
As her arms embrace you, she thanks the Lord above
Look, she's praying. Yes, praying…
For her Father in heaven to bless her with more than enough love for you,
To not foolishly claim that she has all your needs
God gives her the keys and tells her to seek him diligently
In her heart, she promises to stay on her knees
Submitted to sowing in you love's seeds

Wow! Can you see what I see?
Can you believe there is a reality to this dream?
Will your heart allow you to feel life's sweetest treat?
You want love, don't you?
Now tell me, with her, can you see yourself run free?
A woman you can put your arms around and just be
Can you see what I see?
Whenever you're around, the birds sing her harmonies
Can't you see?
Your love releases the woman she's cried out to be

Now tell me… You want love, don't you?

Don't get it twisted. It ain't anything you've put together for her to see
Your physical things won't buy you a minute in this dream
She's been given the vision by God, and this she follows to a tee
Knowing, without him, she'd be easy to mislead
Can you see what I see?
She's got love for you
Submitted her heart and soul to love
Prayed to the heavens above to display love
Sought the Lord day and night for love
So that she could give it away
Blow the man he gives to her into his far way
She's a servant to love
Is encouraged by the spirit to seek out, nurture the seeds of love
And there it was, in the twinkling of your eye
She saw it and knew
So she asked,
"You want love, don't you?"

He's the Amazing Dream That Came True

Matthew's Response to "Baby, Climb with Me"

Baby, I'm climbing with you, if you let me
'Cause I can see this could be our destiny
But I understand...
If you don't see us as a WE

Tempted to press your buttons, but that's not me
Want you to respond, not 'cause of a song
But respond to me for me
Seducing you is not part of my plan...
It needs to be naturally.

Not pressurising you, I'm just enjoying my fantasy
You have been so good to me
I've left it all in God's hands...

Thank God he sent you to me
Accepted staying friends may all this turn out to be
But, my special friend, you will always stay so dear to me
This may look and feel like a fairy tale
So trust the spirit, and go with the heart. It never fails

I feel like I'm living in the book of Songs of Solomon when I'm around you.
You feelin' me?

Donniece Greene-Smith

Matthew's Response to "Make Him More Beautiful"

Truly, Lord, make me more beautiful

Enhance the characteristics that make me even more lovable
I know the love we share will be colourful
Pure and true and, to onlookers, admirable
A love that is not just based on the sexual
But a love that is birthed from the spiritual
A love that also stimulates the mental
A love that satisfies the sensual

Truly, Lord, make me more beautiful

Not forcing my opinions, but always eager to listen
Freely giving my wife everything to me you have given
A heart that is never ceasing in my prayin'
Learning to live life, the way we're supposed to be livin'
SOS! Help! Design me a figure that she will always wanna be lookin'
Give me some recipes, so she can trust me with the cookin'
Oh yeah, Lord, don't forget to teach me good positions for our time of lovemakin'

Truly, Lord, make me more beautiful

He's the Amazing Dream That Came True

You Are Oh So Beautiful

You're oh so beautiful
I better take my time with you
Got me feeling I just wanna get next to you
Still, I need to get to know you
Like Luther, sometimes I get a rush
Feeling, is this too much?
But, man, you are oh so beautiful
And if God says you're the one, I'm gonna get right into you
There is already a natural pull towards you
What's there not to love about you?
There are so many things I'm attracted to
A man with a plan who more than overstands how to treat a lady
My thanks to those who raised you
So assured in your manhood
With you, I feel so understood
You're oh so beautiful
You got me writing and writing pages till I almost got a book full
Meeting you has been so delightful
Darling, with me, you gotta understand
This time, I must follow God's plan
And if you're the man
I will gladly give you my hand
And during our wedding dance
I'll whisper in your ear, "Tonight's the night we go to wonderland"
I'm singing… got me a man that is oh so wonderful

Donniece Greene-Smith

He honours me from head to toe
Respects my inner flow
His character and countenance can stop a show
You're oh so purposeful
Nothing about you makes me feel doubtful
But, instead, I feel oh so joyful
'Cause you're oh so beautiful
Got me feeling all wonderful
Just wanna take a bite full
This night with you is so damn incredible
I'm gonna make sure I give you plentiful
You're gonna feel as though it's unbelievable
We've sowed a harvest of love
And now we have a life full
I'm forever grateful
'Cause I got me a man who's oh so beautiful

He's the Amazing Dream That Came True

His Assurance

Breathe with me,
Come share this moment that was promised to me
Where my heart would get to feel love's sweetest beat
You and I finally
We're not entwined
Just straight up ready to blow each other's minds
No time for games
'Cause to arrive at this place
Was surely pure grace
To be with me, there's no need to chase
My requirement is that you seek the Lord's face
Now my desire seems to have gathered haste
But we will wait, as you assure me love waits
So that when you finally get to enter me
And take a look into my face
You'll see a reflection
Of God's intention
Knowing we will have reached a heavenly place
Still, I'm comforted when you say
For intimacy, we shouldn't race
Your love is assured
When can you put my ring in its rightful space?
For me and my girls, you'll provide a place
Your assurance is morning, noon, and night
You'll be the man of honour I can finally embrace.

Donniece Greene-Smith

He Comforts Me

Would you believe he comforts me?
He's the melody to my beat, he soothes me
My friend, he said, he'll always be
Even if we never become a we
Those were the words he gave to me

My spirit confirms it. That's why I said he comforts me
He does that because he loves me
He's not concerned with time. He waits for me
His words reassure me
That man comforts me

When he says not even a kiss will I steal from thee
Until that day they say you may kiss your bride
I love him so, because I know, in that, he takes pride
He constantly seeks to honour me
He's not afraid to go out on a ledge
Even if love never meets him, and he falls over the edge

His love for me is more than he would've dreamed
What a man!
He'll never make me feel as though he's given in regret
He's a man, and he's after my heart
The way he drops it for me,
Like his love, will never stop

He's the Amazing Dream That Came True

He comforts me
He ain't trying to position me
Or figure me out
He says his job is just to love me
He comforts me
Upholds my thoughts and words, he truly accepts and respects me
He would never mock me
So with his words, he caresses me

I'm feeling aroused, and it's a while before we hit the sheets
God help us
We don't want to race
For, we know, to find each other was pure grace
Still, fill me, although I'm already to the brim
Fill me with desires that pleasure him
This man completes me
He comforts me
His actions to my reaction are always on time
He says his job is to keep me happy
To please me and take away my stress
Saying, "Baby, now that you're with me, you should have rest"
Thank you, Lord, for the man who comforts me
And his burning desire to comfort and please me
His very desire has built a huge fire for him in me
For him, what wouldn't I do?
This wonderful man who comforts me

Donniece Greene-Smith

He Believes in Me

He's constantly trying to encourage me
Not because I'm down. He's just sowing into me
He daily uses words to nourish me
He believes in me

He's got a vision to lift our families
He brings with him love and healing
He's a giver, always looking for ways to bless me
He believes in me

He trusts me
He places his heart, hand, love, and everything most secret into me
With me, he walks fearlessly. Why?
Because he's a man of God, and he believes in me

Every day he tells me how blessed he is to have me
He appreciates me
He thanks the Lord above for me, and so he receives every part of me
He believes in me

Writes a plan on how he wishes to keep me
Tells me love, with us, will be a testimony
He's waited long,
But now, with me, he can write his ultimate love song
All because he believes in me

He's the Amazing Dream That Came True

He tries to understand me, so he can fulfil his plan for us
And think of new ways to increase me
He's got me smiling, glowing
And bringing back every dream I've had of a good man
And calling it reality
'Cause he believes in me

He's looking to add to me
We're planning, documenting, and confessing
Whilst walking and acting out our love-to-be
He understands that if you write the vision, it comes to be
So he's busy preparing for his future with me
Because he believes in me

He's sowing seeds my spirit receives
My heart reads he's in love with me
A harvest grows known or unknown to him
Watered daily, so to him I say, "Love in abundance, here I come"
All because he loves and believes in me

Donniece Greene-Smith

My Wedding Night

What I wanna do wouldn't be right on any other night
That is why I can't wait for my wedding night
The first time for us… I'm sure will be pure delight
I'm lovin' you; you're lovin me
That's got to be, to God, a beautiful sight
Whether you'll slide in as I hold on
Assuring you… for this I have waited so long
I don't know
Not so concerned about the moves, because I know all it will prove
Is when you and I get down into it…
We'll have nothing to lose
How you place your arms that night
Won't matter much as long as they hold me tight
Kiss me right through the night
That will just whet, then whet again my appetite
We've got a lifetime to get this right
Still, on our wedding night, I'm looking to go to great heights
Let us fly that kite
I don't care
Baby, like I said, we've got a lifetime to get this right
Got a unquenchable taste for you
That means the things I wanna do… has got me hungry for you
Can I whet you?
Bless you with that which is watering just for you
Can I feel you?

He's the Amazing Dream That Came True

Can I really feel you?
Can I get to know you?
I hear your plea, "Baby, allow me to be free... we can reach ecstasy"
I hear you saying, "What I wanna do will make you scream"
Grab hold of me
Stop
I can't wait till my wedding night...
Whatever we do, it will be pure delight
We've got a lifetime to get it right... still, I can't wait till my wedding night
Wait we must, though

Donniece Greene-Smith

Matthew's Response to "My Wedding Night"

First Night with a Queen

At the sound of her voice
He stands to attention
Awaiting her next command
Then she beckons him
To enter her private chamber
This was sacred
This was holy
This was an area of her home
Neither of them had ever explored
Excited and anxious, he slowly and carefully slipped right in
His queen ever reassuring him,
"Don't be afraid. It will be OK"
He begins to see the riches
That have been set aside specifically for them
Amazed and thankful for God's grace
Now fully inside, he rocks back and forth in worship
As his being understands he has now entered the most holy place.
His queen also cries out in joy when his worship brings to her more revelation
The room her Father left her
Contains treasures she could have never imagined
She also joins in the worship, rocking back and forth

He's the Amazing Dream That Came True

The experience is incredible
Powerful
Incomparable
It was impossible to halt the worship
He changed his posture
She did too
The worship began once again
And again…
And again…
And again…

Donniece Greene-Smith

I'm Lifted Up on Wings

I'm lifted up on wings every time he thinks of me... it must be
The purest thoughts escape his mind and breathe out loving words to me... constantly
As those words shower me with love, I think this is how it's supposed to be
In my heart, I'm captivated and so submit to everything!
To see the glow of light that reflects the joy inside him is simply blinding
My thoughts... Oh, Lord... You are truly amazing
A dance of passion for me I'm always blessed to see
The question... do I indulge? No second thought... absolutely
Every girl, yes, every girl, dreams this is how love should be
He's not alone in love. He's right beside me
Like the eagles, I wanted to go up higher, so I took to flying
Whispered in his ears, "Come touch the clouds with me"
And he replied, "Funny you should say that. I just bought my wings today"
I hear the critics shout, "You'll fall down. Just wait and see"
Those words could not, would not discourage me
The law of reaping what you sow escaped their mind... unfortunately
And if anything encouraged us more in what we believe
Sow love and sow love and continue to sow love, and before you know it, you will reap abundantly
Have faith and remember... but love, owe no man nothing

He's the Amazing Dream That Came True

Guaranteed nothing, we embrace each day with gratefulness
Leave the world of stress behind, and remember we've been blessed
Walk through the bedroom door, and face the world as one flesh
There's no denying life will bring us moments when were not just trying, but crying
So when it comes to foundation, we use the Lord's cement and keep on designing
You see it's in those seeds… those tiny seeds that make it what it is
No thoughts… of give and see what we get come into it… if we see that spirit, we just bind it
So in this moment in time, we reap more than just blissfulness
His ways of loving me, he makes sure are more than countless
And I'm sowing purposely for a harvest not for me… but just to see him blessed
And in our hearts, they'll never be a shadow of any doubt that God chose for me and him… his best

Donniece Greene-Smith

He Calls Me Up Higher

He's not just whispering sweet somethings
In me, he finds someone to admire
I share my heart with him, and he listens
He finds solutions for all my desires
Oh my God
He calls me up higher

We found each other using our spirit man
Having already walked through a mountain of mire
We're still holding hands
For each other, we hold a huge fire
Diligently sowing seeds so that our love never tires
I call him, and he calls me up higher

He sees the things God has placed in me
I've always wanted, and now I have, a man
Who walks with me. He climbs the mountains with me
Speaks into my visions 'cause he aims to fly with me
And whenever he can't, he tries to be
Understanding I need to grow, he doesn't restrict me
Encouraging me always to follow my dreams
I love him for this and so much more 'cause
He never fails to call me up higher

He's the Amazing Dream That Came True

And just when I think the wooing is over
He's back, showing me how
His love will never tire
No questions asked
I reach out and grab the man that I desire
This love, I'm sure will not expire
As we call each other up higher

Donniece Greene-Smith

Hey, You

Hey, you, I was just meditating on you,
Thought I'd blow a kiss to you
And tell you I'm absolutely head over high heels for you,
Tell me, what should I do?
I really want to be next to you
My vision tells me I have a life with you
My passion grows for you
My desires are for you
Now I just want to spend my days finding ways to please you,
Live out every fantasy I have with you

Hey, you
You make me, you make me
You make me feel so good,
Maybe it's the way you look at me
With your loving eyes, you embrace me
It's like you've discovered treasures
And in your life, you've found nothing that could quite measure

Hey, you. Guess what?
Today I flew to heaven
And asked the angels to help me sing a song for you
Did you hear it?
The wind carried the strings ever so softly
I never knew the angels could take the essence of my heart
And create for you the most perfect song

He's the Amazing Dream That Came True

The harps played "With You Is Where My Heart Belongs" over and over
So tomorrow I'm going back there again

Hey, you
I'm still thinking of you
Put a love message in a bottle and threw it out to sea
Not expecting you to find it
Left it for civilisations in the future to see
Just to give them something to aspire to
An inclination of how much love I have for you

Hey, you
Wanna write the pages to love's history with me?
Help encourage the generation we live in
Seek, sow, and receive love's seed?
In this, I feel a need

Hey, you
Will you walk with me?
Maybe talk a little with me
Write some beautiful love songs with me
The ones that'll play when love is in the air

Hey, you
Look what I've found

Donniece Greene-Smith

A cloud we could float on
He says his name is nine
And a ride on him
Will take us to another time

Hey, you
I'm gonna close my eyes now and go to sleep
And pray that my eyes get another opportunity tomorrow to say
Hey, you

He's the Amazing Dream That Came True

His Eyes Compose the Scores

*His eyes compose the scores that daily capture my heart
With his fingers, he translates the melodies that almost make my heart stop
Creating for the world and I symphonies so sweet
His care for me generates ardour for him
Giving me visions of ways to delight him
Who is he? He's my Mr. Me,
Everybody should know by now he's the amazing dream that came true for me
My darling, my lover,
He is my king
My thoughts are filled with a constant longing to honour him
Make all the money I can and pamper him
Take him around the world and fine wine and dine him
Let him feel the love I create every morning
Then spend the day showering him
He's not wondering how this could be
The law that you reap what you sow has guided him
A prayer and his faith led the seeds he's placed in me
Knowing this has driven me
To the God of abundance
To thank him for my gift
Matthew Nathaniel Smith
And in God's choice for me, I rest assuredly
Confident he's placed a man of faith right in front of me*

Donniece Greene-Smith

Into him I sow love diligently
As he plants his seeds in me unselfishly
Knowing… but not needing to demand, he reaps abundantly
As Christ so loved the church, he gave his life for all eternity
And every day, I mean every day, a near enough love through him visits me.

She Hears a Whisper in the Wind

She hears a whisper in the wind that's carried to her, saying,
"I wonder how comes she loves me,
I wonder exactly what could it be,
What makes her want to be with me?"
So she breathes in the direction of the wind
And says, "Tell him it's the way he looks at me,
And how, with his words, he nourishes me."
His encouragement lifts me.
I love the way he constantly seeks to honour me.
That alone excites me.
It makes me want to fulfil all his marital fantasies.
Oh, how his character blesses me.
When I think of him, I can't stop smiling.
I know, in him, is where my true love with a man will begin.
Never have I ever felt such bliss, and we haven't even shared a kiss.
Now hurry wind, as these words I wouldn't want him to miss
And he whispers back, "Thank you for loving me."

Donniece Greene-Smith

I Flew Past Your Heart Today

I flew past your heart today and
Blew you the most unbelievable kiss
If you felt it, you would've felt
All the wonderful thoughts
And wishes I have for you
You would've smiled at the thought
Of my touch, which is packed
With such amazing feelings for you
Love like this doesn't grow
In just any old heart
But it's been seeded with a desire
To go the distance
So, realising love has no boundaries
I find myself on an endless road
In a river that has no bottom
With a passion that can bring
The faintest heart to life
So it was
As I flew past your heart today

Going Heights with You

Every time I think about it
I go all goo-goo
But it's true
When we make love, I climb spiritual heights with you
I really get into you
Kissing everything in sight
It gets so intense, I can't help but bite you
Sh** I'm enjoying you
Just wanna love every part of you
Is this what they call marital bliss?
When is the next time I'm so excited
You gotta come and get some of this
You mean to tell me, all my life, this is what I've missed?
Ever so gentle you are
How does one describe the feeling of you inside?
Is this heaven? I can't decide.
All I know is, when you and I climax
My sweetest moment is realising it's with you
Every time just gets better with you
The way you make love is beautiful
Can we take our time with this?
Learn to master expressing sexual bliss
When I'm in your arms, I feel so privileged
I feel like you're the first man on Earth, and I'm the only woman
My eyes and heart see no one else here

Donniece Greene-Smith

And if there was, they couldn't compare
The best part is my desire to constantly please you
Create endless passion from my dreams for you
This woman wants to become all she can with you
Baby, I look forward to spending my life going heights with you.

He's the Amazing Dream That Came True

Come with Me

Let me lie on your chest
Don't matter if it's back to chest, or chest to breast
When we're finally flesh to flesh, my heart will rest
Your loving I haven't tasted, but my spirit says, for me, it is the best
Our promise to each other is
I'll never regret putting on my wedding dress
I feel so blessed,
Baby, make love to me now. Relieve my stress
From all my years of settling for less
Of never having love that took away my breath
It just doesn't get any better than this
We'll both say, at last, we've found bliss
My lips, and anything else you want, please kiss
Whatever we miss
We can do it again. I'm in no hurry
For all our fantasies will make the bucket list
I wanna love you
Do all the things you need me to
Baby, I'm looking forward to pleasing you
Scream out for you. Oh… I know I'll scream out for you
Wanting more of you, so much more of you
My ecstasy will be me and you in the bedroom… free
If your loving sends me out of Earth,
Come with me, please. Please, come with me
When I'm shivering, wrap me in your arms

Donniece Greene-Smith

Tell me how much it means to you
If you've got the strength, ease right in and then
Take me to the moon again
However many times, I'm just glad I'm with you
Can't wait to show you
I wanna climb the mountain with you
Fly the kite of real good loving with you
And feel the passion running through you
Honey, I love you
And living out each moment with you is my dream come true.

He's the Amazing Dream That Came True

All I See Is Beauty-full

Closed my eyes and felt my way to you
Overcame my fears as I'm supposed to
Then pushed back thoughts that seemed to deny you
With love on my mind, it was so easy to do
My trust in God was exercised in letting him choose you
For he alone knew
How I would find a life full of love with you
I'm now living out dreams with you
Matthew, when I look at you
All I see is beauty-FULL
That's why it was easy to say, "I do"
I never have an emotion I can't share with you
Won't hold none of this love back if they pay me to
Every year, I'll renew my vows and remarry you
I now walk out my dreams and climb the tree of reality with you
Never alone, in love, I fly with you
Heaven is where I'll take you
Tell me, what shall we do?
How does being a daddy sound to you?
Maybe God will bless us with a baby or two
If I have my wish, he'll give us a son just like you
Beautiful brown eyes that melt me like the sweetest dew
Matthew, when I look at junior you
All I see is beauty-FULL
He's the blessing that came from you

Donniece Greene-Smith

And surely he will follow you
Gentle yet strong, he's promised to be purposeful
Hey Matthew, more than yesterday, I'm more in love with you
Looking forward to tomorrow and the rest of my life with you
'Cause with you, all I see is beauty-FULL!

He's the Amazing Dream That Came True

Every Moment with You

*I tried to find the words that best describe my emotion
And in my search, the words I've now accepted are endless
Slightly frustrated, because I wanted my words to paint a picture
Or maybe capture the essence of what I was feeling
And every time I looked back at a moment that touched me
There flashed another word across my memory
Although very beautiful, I couldn't understand how
What I was looking for appeared to always change
In my back and forth with my mind, I asked, "Don't you get it?"
I just want to take a picture and maybe write a note or two
Describing how every moment is when I'm with you
Then it dawns on me like the sweetest hug
It's not about describing as much as it is about being in the moment
So I give up my search now and just embrace every moment with you.*

Donniece Greene-Smith

I'm Gonna Love You Now

I'm gonna love you now
For tomorrow is not all it's cracked up to be
Although you are not here
My heart still finds emotions in words as though you are near
So my breath I shall not spare
I send my love in a whisper, delivered on the wind, straight to your ear
My dear, can you hear?
Thoughts of you release excitement my body tries to bear
And with you there is no fear
Today's love for you leaves yesterday's behind... 'cause it just can't compare
Can you feel me, although I'm not there?
I've seen our hearts next meeting, and it's joy they both share
The sun reflects your smile in my glance
Still, you're not in my presence
Yet anticipation takes things up a gear
Oh, I felt a shiver, something like when you run your fingers through my hair
We do make a beautiful pair
In my tomorrow, I won't promise to care
For tomorrow is not all it's cracked up to be
So I'm gonna love you now.

Of All the Days with You

Of all the days with you,
This one is the best.
Yesterday was a blast,
But that is now in the past.
This day is so spectacular,
I had to write on the steamy bathroom glass and tell you,
And the happy face is because I'm still with you.
Did I tell you I love your hands?
Especially when they're holding me.
Shall we dance?
When I lean into you, everything is enhanced.
Is this what they call romance?
On this, everyone should take a chance,
But then that wouldn't be allowing others to have their experiences,
So let me focus on me and this beautiful day,
'Cause knowing I'm with you is all that matters.

Donniece Greene-Smith

At Long Last, Your Arms Found Me

At long last, your arms found me
And from this day on, I pray to never be free
Only you were meant to hold me
Like sandpaper to wood, I use your love to help mould me

Every thought of you has proven true
In my inexhaustible imagination, I sit and ponder on how your affections are like sweet dew
So gentle yet reaching in all the right places
Touching my heart but caressing my mind
Darling, your words always seem to be on time

You were created in what is known as eternity's past age
Then translated spiritually onto my page
Where, through my breath, were you and I given life
I put pen to paper in order to describe your beauty and how it blessed me
And I am thankful for surrendering trust to my creator who delivered you to me

You will always be the gift straight out of God's hand
That's how I see you—his best man
And now I attempt to write pages so the world will understand
How, through our open hearts, we live this spiritual romance

He's the Amazing Dream That Came True

Hopefully, through these writings, they will get a glance

No one can deny this love of mine a place in history
He stands amongst the greatest men you've ever seen
His love is regal, yet in his giving, he is most humble
His flaws are but small stones in a pile of rocks
Adding believable dimensions to his majestic armour

My love, my dream come true
I've imprisoned myself in love only to serve you
For forever and a day, I'm lavished with your love. I am not only thankful but grateful
To every moment in the past, which brought you into today's view, Matthew "I love you."

Donniece Greene-Smith

Your Love

In your mind are the purest of thoughts
Never failing to think of me wholesomely
In your eyes is the clearest of vision
Always seeing me with love's clarity
With loving gazes, you paint the most beautiful canvas of me
And in your words are melodies, revealing secrets
With which you sing beautiful words to me
Constantly you are adding to me
Massaging your affections into my mentality
In your arms, you encourage intimacy
Showing excitement and zeal to everything I reveal
It's no doubt that your touch releases in me rivers
Of unending waters, beckoning you unto me
Your love eagerly anticipating, assured "it" I will receive
Moments of ecstasy never leave me wondering
In you, I already believe
From the moment God's vision became real to me
Becoming one with you was sealed in our destiny

He's the Amazing Dream That Came True

With Love You Always Win

With me you dared to be
Although disapproving opinions, direct and discreet, surfaced at the thought of we
You allowed nothing to come in the way of us being
This would become one of those stories written about
Where all the great opposing bodies would fall
Religion, pride, and prejudice in all their efforts to stand tall
Would discover what we have come to know… that love conquers all

And through this experience, Love would show us its perfect resolve
As your valiant steps towards Love would miraculously open many other doors
Showing us the way to triumph by staying calm through the many storms
Where we would enjoy the rewards and benefits for our faithfulness
As Love does what it does
It's always made clear its intention to us who submitted to its unbounded ways
Its call was for us to experience wonders that we have only witnessed in dreams
Not needing consent from others, Love asked us to go heights with it

Donniece Greene-Smith

Unveiling the splendour God had placed within us

The journey towards surrendering would be liberating
If we could reach beyond things considered trifling
Like fault-finding and measuring one's means
Love would unveil qualities within each other that were worth treasuring
As Love reveals, with me you always win
It's true
Spiritually it's as if I've walked eternities with you
And I'm enjoying learning so much about you

A long way now we are from the sounding brass
Hallelujah… Love's river has sailed us to still waters at long last
Where we savour fruits from seeded good intentions of past
A million more seeds we'd sow for Love. In fact, we'd do whatever Love asked

www.ingramcontent.com/pod-product-compliance
Ingram Content Group UK Ltd.
Pitfield, Milton Keynes, MK11 3LW, UK
UKHW041228200426
11947UKWH00034B/440